Toy is from Thailand

For Nizz

Printed in the United States of America

First Printing: July 2009

ISBN-13: 978-1439250389
ISBN-10: 1439250383

Toy is from Thailand

Written and illustrated by Whitney Badgett

Sawadee,

My name is Ittipon, but everyone calls me Toy.
In Thailand, most children are called by their nicknames.
I live in a teakwood house in Bangkok, the capital of Thailand, with my mom, dad, and little sister Lek.

Sawadee: (Sah-wah-dee) Hello

Teakwood comes from a tall, yellowish-brown tree known for its strength and weather resistance, and is often used for shipbuilding and furniture.

A spirit house is a small model of a home or temple, usually found in every yard in Thailand. The spirits believed to live there protect the home and are given daily offerings of food, water, and flowers.

My sister and I go to school five days a week. My dad takes us to school on his motorcycle. On the way, we pass all sorts of different vehicles: buses, cars, trucks, motorized food stands, and tuk tuks.

A tuk - tuk (took - took) is a colorful, three-wheeled motorized taxi used throughout Thailand for transportation.

When I arrive at school, I wai to my teacher to show respect. In Thailand, that's how people greet each other. We learn about many different subjects, including reading and writing the Thai language. The Thai alphabet has 44 different letters.

The wai is the traditional Thai greeting performed by placing the palms of your hands together in front of your face. It can be used to say hello, thank you, sorry, or to show respect.

For lunch at school, we usually have spicy food. Most of the time, I eat rice for every meal. I drink fresh coconut milk, or eat some juicy Thai fruit for snacks like rambutan or durian, which has a spiky green peel and a very strong odor. Some Thai people eat fried bugs for a snack. Aloy!

A rambutan (rahm-byu-tahn) is a small, sweet, white fruit with a red peel that has soft, whitish yellow spikes.

Thai people often fry and eat insects such as grasshoppers, silkworm cocoons, and bamboo worms.

Aloy: (ah-loy) delicious

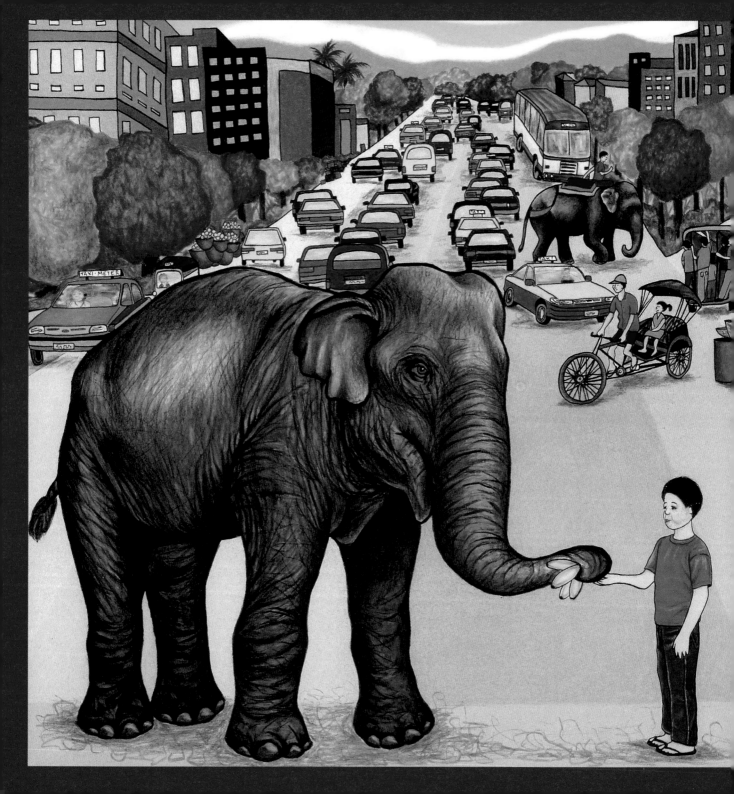

Sometimes when I'm on the way home from school, I see an elephant walking down the street. Usually, there is a man riding it who sells bananas. I like to buy some and feed the elephant. Most elephants have reflectors tied behind their tails to keep them safe walking through the traffic.

A motorized food stand is a motorcycle or bicycle with a food stand attached to it in some way. As they weave in and out of traffic, often ringing bells to attract customers, they sell desserts, hot dogs, fruit, vegetables, and even spicy meals.

My family practices the Buddhist religion, like most other Thai people. Every morning my mother prepares an offering of fresh flower garlands and rice for Buddha. She also gives food every morning to the monks walking by our house with their alms bowls.

Flower garlands are made of jasmine, red roses, or purple orchids sewn together with a needle and thread.

The purpose of an alms bowl is to receive an offering of food.

Soon, I will become a Buddhist monk novice for a few weeks, as most Thai boys do at least once in their life. I will shave my head, wear an orange robe, and study the principles of Buddhist teaching. Some people decide to be a monk for the rest of their lives.

Mai pen rai (mai-peh-lai) means nevermind, and is the most common phrase in Thailand. The phrase reflects the friendly, relaxed attitude of Thai people.

On the weekend, I visit my grandma and grandpa who are rice farmers in the country. Rice is the main crop of Thailand and is planted at the beginning of the rainy monsoon season. I like to go outside and visit their water buffalo that help plow the rice fields. Afterwards, my grandma cooks my favorite lunch with som tam, fried chicken, and sticky rice.

A monsoon is a seasonal wind that brings heavy rainfall.

Som tam (sum-tahm) is a popular Thai salad made with green papaya, garlic, sugar, fish sauce, hot peppers, string beans, lime juice and dried shrimp.

My grandpa enjoys watching Thai boxing, the most popular sport in Thailand. My sister would rather watch classical Thai dancing. She practices bending her fingers back as part of the special dance, and she admires their colorful costumes made of Thai silk. Both boxing and dancing are accompanied by Thai classical musicians.

The sound of Thai classical music has been compared to a stream or river. It has a soft, steady melody with smaller melodies blending in and out.

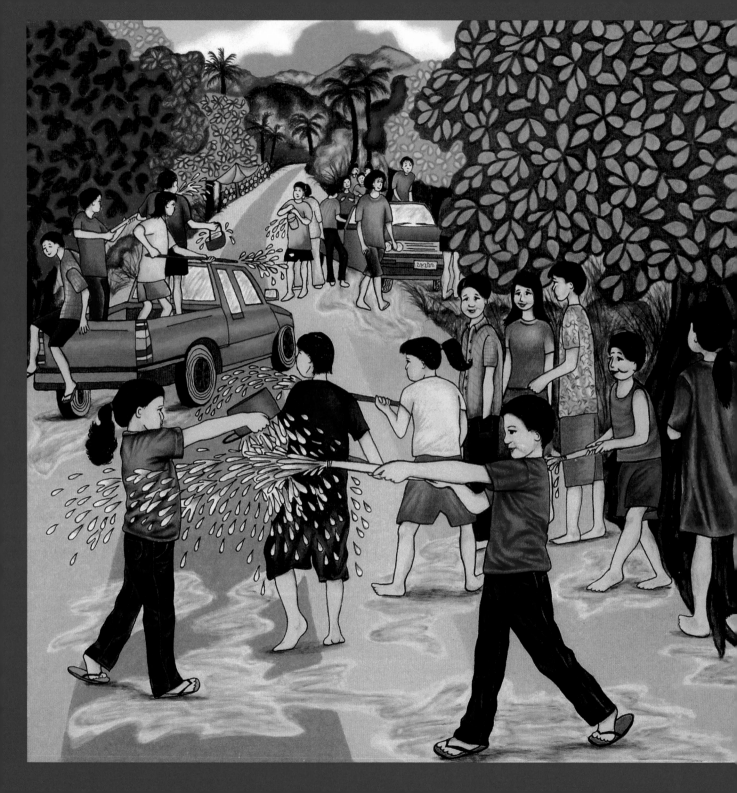

My favorite holiday is the Thai New Year, which takes place in April. Thailand is hot all year, but is the hottest during the months of March and April. As the New Year arrives, everyone in the entire country cools off in a three-day water fight.

The Thai calendar is based on the Buddhist calendar, so the New Year takes place in April rather than January. For example, the year 2009 is actually 2552 in Thailand.

Besides New Year, there are many occasions to celebrate. On one special day, Thailand lights up for the king's birthday. Everyone loves the king and queen, and the cities and villages are filled with flowers, lights, and photographs to honor them.

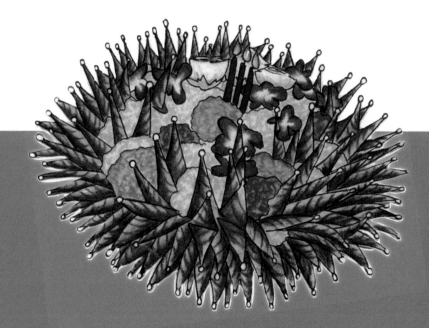

Loy Krathong (loy-gah-toeng) is another holiday in Thailand, which takes place on the night of the twelfth full moon of the year. To celebrate the end of the monsoon season and to welcome the harvest season, people send flower wreath rafts with candles in the center floating down the rivers.

I am happy to live here in the Land of Smiles with my family. There is always a coconut to drink, and there are many fun things to do. And you never know where or when you might spot an elephant or a monkey!

One city in Thailand, Lopburi, hosts an annual monkey party, full of food and fun for the estimated 600 monkeys that live near them.

In the past, there were many canals in Bangkok on which people traveled and traded their goods. Floating markets can still be seen today, as people float up and down some canals on boats selling fruit, vegetables, and other products.

Made in the USA
Monee, IL
20 August 2020